How To Lighten The Heavy Load of Fibromyalgia

To order additional copies, please contact us.
BookSurge, LLC
www.booksurge.com
1-866-308-6235
orders@booksurge.com

How To Lighten The Heavy Load of Fibromyalgia

My Personal Journey & My Road to Recovery

Karen S. Grove

Publisher

2003

How To Lighten The Heavy Load of Fibromyalgia

Table of Contents

Introduction

I Know What It Feels Like To Have Fibromyalgia

I have been a Fibromyalgia sufferer since 1992. It is a debilitating disease and it takes the life that you had away from you. It affects every morsel of your being. The flu-like symptoms are sometimes overwhelming, not to mention the complications and havoc that it plays on every part of your body. It is still unknown what causes Fibromyalgia so we are treated for the symptoms with medication and pray every day that someone will find the cause.

While we are waiting, many of us take numerous medications to ease the pain, the depression, and the sleepless nights. I did. This baggage is a heavy load to carry. We drag it around with us and just cannot quite figure out what to do with it. Hopefully, after you have read this book, you will be more enthused and excited to try my self-invented system called THE GROVE APPROACH: HEALTHIER LIVING WITH FIBROMYALGIA.

Just know that you are not alone. One in every twenty-seven people in the United States suffers from this disease. Based on my own experience, I feel strongly that my balanced program will help you live a better quality life. All of the materials for the program are offered on my website at www.thegroveapproach.com.

Please visit me, not just once, but as often as you need to. Stay in touch and most of all try to stay positive.

This Book Is Dedicated To All Of My Family And Friends Who Have Supported Me Through The Tough Times In Life And To Those Who Celebrate A Brighter Life With Me Now.

I.

My Traumatic Entrance into This World

My journey of life started in October of 1954. I was a pudgy and "not so cute" baby. Those were my Mom's words after thirty-six long hours of labor. I was a breech baby and back in those days they did not do caesarian sections. They turned me to try to get my head in normal position for birth. I was a very stubborn child and they finally delivered me "feet first". I have always liked my feet planted firmly on the ground. I am still that way but sometimes life does not cooperate. I think that is what they call "Living and Learning." Oh boy, have I had experience in that department!

I weighed in at nine pounds and was 21-½" long. This was very large for those days. Fortunately I did not stay large, speaking from a woman's point of view. My baby years were pretty normal. My Mom was a stay-at-home Mom and I really liked that.

My Nana had a huge influence in my life. She taught me how to sew. She taught me how to play the piano and she comforted me when I was scared or upset. Having her in my life for eight years was a tremendous bonus for me.

I lived in rural Pennsylvania. There were no street lights and going to town was a wonderful treat. It was definitely a sheltered life in many ways but sometimes I still was not protected from the world outside. You will learn more about that later in my book.

I loved the farm. My kittens were my world. I fed them bottles, cared for them, and doted over them. I am sure the mother of each litter just wanted me to go away!

My brother and I were very close and we still are. We rode ponies together, made mud hamburgers, played in our tree house, and we sometimes fought. We really were very normal children.

Most of our fights revolved around a bright red tricycle that my mother purchased at the Salvation Army. We were so proud of that tricycle. We hated to share it so we would race to eat our dinner. The first one done would ask to be excused from the table and race out to the bike and hide it from the other. If we hadn't spent so much time hiding it from each other, we would have had so much more riding time, but that was not the sensible thing to do at the time.

We each had our daily chores and I am so glad that my parents raised us that way. It gave us a sense of responsibility very early in life. Farm living was not easy. We didn't get to go on very many vacations. I am not complaining though, because it made every little thing we did so special. Trips to the Dairy Supreme were just so special. Once a summer we would go to an amusement park locally. Every July 4th, we went as a family to the local drive-in theatre. These are all good things that I remember from my childhood.

The problem is that it only takes one bad experience to ruin those precious days. My next chapter describes my bad experience and how I handled it through life.

Before I go on, I would like to end each chapter with a little humorous story. One evening my family and I were all sitting around the table looking at family photos and we got the movie projector out and watched the old 8mm movies of every childhood Christmas. There was something very consistent about all of the photos of me. I did not notice it but my brother noticed and started to laugh hysterically. What could be that funny? Well, sure enough, every time I had my photo taken, I would wet my pants. In every picture and movie, I had this big dark spot on my overalls. It gave us all a good laugh. It feels good to laugh. I try to find something good to laugh about in every situation, no matter how bad it is.

2.

A Childhood Experience That You Never Forget

I was four very young years old when my bad experience started. At least, that is when I remember it starting. Even though we did not spend much time away from the farm, a person that was supposed to be a friend to the family found plenty of time to spend with me. It was not "quality time" to say the least. This man made an impression on me that has been the footprint of my life for over forty-six years. He was a kind man, or so I thought at that age. He paid attention to me and he wanted to take me everywhere with him.

After he got comfortable with me, he started to touch me in places that I knew were private areas. It was a gradual process but eventually it became a common thing when I was with him. He told me that I was being a bad girl and if I told anyone I would be punished. Of course, at the age of four, I believed him and never told anyone until about eight years ago.

Carrying the secret was so difficult. I was robbed of my childhood. When the others were playing, I felt like I should not be. I should be punished because I was a bad girl. I wondered why he was the only man that did these things. No other man ever tried to do these things. Was there something wrong with me?

I wondered this through my childhood years and never felt like I fit in. I always felt different than the other children and I guess I was. I just did not know how to handle it so I blocked it out of my mind as much as I could. I was afraid of men. I was a bed wetter until I was eight years old. This was so humiliating because if I stayed over at anyone's house, my mom had to explain and I was so embarrassed.

I had no idea the impact that this would have on my life throughout the years. The man died when I was about eight and I was never so glad to see a lid close on a casket. I thought that the memories would die with him, but they did not.

There is a reason for telling you this personal and very private story. I did not realize the impact it had on every aspect of my life until I got sick with Fibromyalgia. One of the questions that the doctor first asked me was, "Had I ever been touched or molested as a child?" I was so shocked when he asked and I was so relieved to finally be able to say, "Yes, yes I was."

Finally, another human being knew that deep dark secret and I was able to bring it to the surface and deal with it. It felt good to get it out and it is much easier to talk about now that I understand that I wasn't a bad child. He was a sick man.

Sometimes we hide things in our mind and think they are not affecting us, but they really are and this really affected me so much until I sorted through it with the doctor. Your deep dark secret may not be the same as mine, but I encourage you to unload any suppressed baggage. You will feel so much better and it helps the healing process, not only emotionally, but physically as well.

I pray that none of you ever went through anything like this, but if you did, I encourage you to share it with a person that you trust or a trained professional counselor.

3.

The Teen Years Were Cruel

Starting Junior High was an emotional and traumatic adjustment. There were more students because two schools within the district combined at this point. It was fun to get to know other people but at the same time it was quite overwhelming. Suddenly, the world and the friends that you shared for six years were blended into a group that doubled in size.

This was a point when dating started for many students. My parents were a bit more strict. I had to be sixteen to officially go out on a date. I was so relieved. I really did not want anything to do with dating and this gave me an excuse.

After my traumatic experience as a child, boys really scared me. I thought that they would only want to go out because they wanted to have sex. I was still very immature and very scared of that thought.

I was very religious and I felt that sex was something that you waited to have after you got married. That was definitely not the rule of thumb for most of the people that I knew. I didn't understand why they would want to give their body to someone that they were not sure they were going to share the rest of their life with.

As you can imagine, I was labeled untouchable, unfriendly, mysterious, scaredy pants, party pooper, and the list went on.

I did not drink or smoke so that eliminated me from invitations to very many parties. That was ok with me. It just helped me to avoid awkward situations. If I was friends with someone and they chose to drink or smoke, I just found a new friend.

I can name three true friends that I went through my high school years with. Their values and beliefs were very similar to mine. We had fun but not drinking, smoking, or having sex. We had fun shopping, we all liked to sew, we were all musical, and we just enjoyed one another's company.

In my junior year, I met a boy. I was definitely smitten with his looks, his charm and the fact that he was the first boy that I ever felt comfortable with. He respected my values and he understood my wishes as far as sex was concerned. There weren't very many boys as understanding as he was. I thought he was the one.

We dated off and on through my junior year but his eyes were always wandering and I wondered if he was truly happy. I didn't say anything because when you are that age, losing a boyfriend was like failing your driver's license test!

Between my junior and senior year, things started to change for me. I felt comfortable talking to boys and I started to branch out and meet new people. I thought this was what my friend wanted also, but he came to me and asked if we could go steady. That was the term for it back then.

I was so happy and could not see anything but us being together for the rest of our lives. We did everything together, so I thought. What I did not know until I read his journal was that he had feelings for someone else. This broke my heart. I never brought it up. It would have been the end of the world to lose him. After all, he did not make me meet any sexual expectations. I just felt that there was no one else out there who would allow me that freedom.

We continued to date during my senior year. He had already graduated and was working for his father in their family painting business. I really never asked him if he ever saw the other person. I really did not want to know. My self-esteem was so low from my childhood experience, that to start all over in the dating process would have been a nightmare.

When it was time to pick a college, I chose a college close to home. He wanted me to be close and I wanted to stay close. I guess there was a sense of mistrust, but I would have never admitted that to him or anyone at the time. I graduated from high school and the next step would be college.

There is a lighter side to this whole teen experience that I would like to share because everything that I am writing is to make you think of your situations and to see if you can draw out any possible traumatic events or experiences that would have built up to cause the onset of Fibromyalgia.

There was a family that lived around the corner from us. They were different from most families because they had seven boys! Right, there were seven mischievous boys. And the ones that were close to my age did everything in their power to trick, haunt, and taunt me. They really did watch out for me through the years, but it is truly a wonder I am still alive.

The funniest thing that ever happened was when their son that was closest in age to me found out that my boyfriend was two-timing me. He set up camp at my house. I asked him what he thought he was going to prove. He told me to wait and watch.

Well, sure enough, my boyfriend came to the door and there sat this guy, very handsome and very eligible. But we were too close to be a couple. We were more like brother and sister. The only thing was that my boyfriend did not know that. This guy just sat perched while my boyfriend squirmed.

He was not budging. My boyfriend got mad, took a bunch of forks, and proceeded to stick every fork in the watermelon sitting on the kitchen table. He was very frustrated and then he left. We sat and just giggled and laughed like little kids. That is what true friends are for, right?

4.

The College Dream

I decided to stay in the area because I chose to be closer to my boyfriend. The choice was right for me at the time. I started college in September of 1972. My major was Elementary Education. Children were always part of my life and I just dreamed of the chance to teach young children. There is nothing more rewarding than seeing the light bulb come on or a happy face because of something they learned from a teacher.

I think that going to school and living at home was very difficult. I still felt like I was in high school. The demands were higher in the family life department. I was expected to participate in all family gatherings, even if I had important work to do for school.

The demands were high because my boyfriend and I saw each other most every evening. This made studying a more difficult task and took major planning. My boyfriend did help me study and he did help me with projects, but I still felt like something was missing from the college experience.

Many times I thought of transferring to another school. I worked on the farm through my entire first three years of college. I did not get summers off. That is when most of the work was done on the farm. It was busy every summer.

The summer after my sophomore year, my boyfriend proposed to me. We decided to be married in May of 1975. This would be after my junior year was finished and it would be the summer before I student taught.

I feel like I missed out on many of social experiences in college that I should have had before I got married but these years were probably about the most stable years that we had together, to my knowledge anyway.

Let me tell you a story that will make you laugh until you cannot laugh anymore. Any woman will appreciate this one.

It was a snowy day in November, my third year at college. It was that wet sticky snow, the kind that you like to use for making snowmen. It was cold and damp and I had to walk several blocks from class to class. I was a commuter and I guess the university thought that exercise was the key to success because I probably walked over two miles a day just getting to and from classes.

This particular day was like any other. I had ten minutes to get from my first class to the Science building where my second class was. There was not enough time to move the car, so I walked, or rather I ran, to class.

As I was running, it felt like a weight on my one leg was pulling along with me. I thought to myself, "Wow, are you ever out of shape. It feels like I am carrying a ball and chain." Only, I knew that I wasn't. I looked down and I was dragging a big ball of snow along with me.

You are probably wondering how this could have been. So was I. After further investigation, I realized that a pair of pantyhose must have been mixed in with my jeans in the wash and were stuck on the inside of my pant leg. As I ran, I was gathering a snowman!

You can just imagine how I felt. Like a blooming idiot. With many eyes on me, of course, I proceeded to very casually pick up the pantyhose. I walked over to the trash can and threw them in just as if I were throwing a piece of paper away.

My only hope was that I never saw any of those people again, ever. But we all know the odds of that were close to zero because they came and went to the same classes I did. Oh well, just a little humor to let you all know that there is no such thing as perfection.

5.

Marriage: To Have and to Hold Forever

I was married in May of 1975. Marriage was forever to me. Saying vows in front of two hundred friends and family and God was a forever commitment to me. I celebrated the first day of the rest of my life with the man that would share our dreams, our sorrows, our successes, our happiness, and hopefully our children someday. At least that is what I thought.

Marriage was good to us. He had a wonderful job and I eventually took a full-time job working at a local bank. We were living on a budget, but we still went out on weekends to movies and dinner. We had toys and we had a beautiful home.

Our first summer as newlyweds was a wild summer. We were making a new home for ourselves. I was working with the painting crew at a local college with his family. I tucked away enough money to pay for my senior year of college.

The summer went very fast and before I knew what hit me, I was student teaching in a kindergarten class in the area. I enjoyed it so much and I just loved teaching.

My second half of student teaching was with a fifth grade class in the area. They came to me for Social Studies and that was just a wonderful experience.

I felt distanced from my husband because I was so involved with the student teaching experience. Not only was I gone all day, but the preparation time doing bulletin boards, lesson plans, games, etc. was endless. There just were not enough hours in the day!

I finished my last semester by taking the final classes that I needed to graduate. Graduation Day was a special day for me and my family. I was the only child in our family of five children to get a college degree. This was a big deal to my parents.

My mother wanted to do something special for me. She invited my family and my husband's entire family for a wonderful dinner after my graduation. It was so sad. No one showed up except my family and my husband. Not one of his six brothers and sisters came. His parents never acknowledged why they did not come. This was the first of many experiences which I had with his family that made strong statements about how they felt about me. That is how I viewed it anyway.

When my mother sat crying, it hurt me so much. When she hurt, I hurt. She was a special person and she tried as hard as I did to please their family. It just seemed that they really did not care. I kept the hurt within our family and went on with life. This was the end of my college days and the beginning of my "real world" experience.

I worked as a substitute teacher for two years. I did many long-term substitute jobs but I never got a full-time teaching job. After two years, I needed some stability and I needed to know that I was going to work every day. I applied at a local bank. I was hired in 1978 and worked there until April of 1980.

We decided to start a family in the summer of 1979. I got pregnant right away. The pregnancy was uneventful, although I felt like I was carrying around a bowling ball. I really enjoyed being pregnant.

Our first son was born in April of 1980. He weighed almost nine pounds but he did not give me a hard time like I gave my mother during labor and delivery. His birth was very easy and suddenly we were the proud parents of a baby boy. OK, now I was ready to know how to be a parent. Where was the script for that?

I really do not think that either of us was ready for all of the parenting surprises. The first day that I brought him home, I nursed him and you can probably guess what happened next. A nursing baby explodes when they have a bowl movement. No one warned me about this.

I called my husband in from outside to help me. By the time he got there, I had every towel dirty and almost a full box of wipes dirty. It was a mess but a happy mess.

No one prepared us for sleepless nights when the baby did not feel good or just wanted to be up. No one said anything about a crying baby that just got tummy aches all the time. I could see that I had to spend all my time with the baby and I know that my husband felt neglected but the baby came first. This was the first time that I ever picked up the phone and called my mother to just say "thanks".

Thanks for taking care of me for all of those years when I was a child.

Being a stay-at-home mom was different. I enjoyed it but at the same time I missed the interaction with people my own age. Every morning, my husband got to leave and go be with adults. I guess I resented his leaving every morning but I did not say anything. Instead, our evening conversations were about what new things the baby did that day, how many times he smiled and, of course, how many times he pooped! There was not very much adult conversation between us anymore. I felt us drifting away from what was going on in our lives.

I decided that I would like to return to work on a part-time basis. I called the bank where I had worked and they were very receptive. They would work my hours around my schedule and not give me any more than twenty hours per week. This sounded perfect until my husband got home from work that night.

He shot me down like a row of ducks at the carnival! He wondered what the point would be. He said that I would not make any money after I paid a babysitter so I might as well stay home. The part that he did not understand was that I needed to work for interaction with adults. I was not going back to make money.

After many discussions, I felt that I should do what he thought was right. I chose to stay home with the baby. I found plenty to do. Gardening was enjoyable for me. I mowed the lawn, kept the house, and did all of the mother and wife duties that I felt I was supposed to do.

Something was missing. It seemed that everything I did, my husband re-did. I mowed the lawn wrong, so he would re-mow it. I did the dishes wrong, so he would re-do them, showing me places that I missed on them. I felt so small and I had such low self-esteem. He belittled me physically. I only weighed 108 pounds, not much to belittle. I had terrible problems with my skin after my son was born. The doctor said it was hormone changes and I took medication every day. My husband told me that if I would just wash my face once in a while, it would help.

I just could not seem to please him. We decided to have another baby. I thought that would please him, so in the fall of 1981, I was pregnant again. Our second son was also almost nine pounds, a very easy delivery, and a wonderful baby. I think that I was much more relaxed and the baby sensed it.

I loved having the two boys. We went everywhere together. My favorite thing was to dress them alike and have their pictures done. That worked until they were about six and eight years old. At this point, they said no more of this!

I really had just started to settle into our family life when I realized there was something terribly wrong in our marriage. My husband was coming home late, he was not where he said he was going to be, and patterns started to develop which spelled trouble for us.

After I found out what was going on, I called our pastor to set up counseling. He said that he would go with me. We worked for over one year to try to mend damages, but the damage still continued.

My husband moved out of the house in August of 1983. He asked to move back in November of 1983. I allowed him with conditions attached. He knew the consequences if those conditions and promises were broken.

One very cold January night, I sat on the couch waiting for him to come home. As time went by, I just felt a sick feeling in my stomach. I hoped that he had not been in an accident, but I really felt that I knew what was happening.

As I sat in the dark, his truck pulled in around 11:00 PM. I surprised him because the room was dark and I think that I scared him when he came in. I asked one question and he gave the answer that changed my life for good. The next morning, I filed for divorce.

In March of 1984, the boys and I moved to a two bedroom apartment in town. It was a darling apartment and very comfortable. I actually slept so well knowing there was some peace and finality to our situation. Of course, my husband said that no one would ever want me after having two children. He also told me that I would never make it on my own. I guess that I have proved him wrong!

6.

Working and Being a Single Parent

The next years were difficult. The boys were passed back and forth on weekends. I worked at a job where I loved the work but where my boss was verbally abusive. We had very little money and I was suddenly alone as an adult, thinking of getting back into the dating scene. This was a position that I never dreamed of being in.

I had very little confidence in myself at that time. My ex-husband had really done a number on me and then I had a new boss that was doing the same thing. It seemed that no-one just accepted me for who I was. Who was I? I was about to find out.

This was the time in my life when I became my own person. I probably had a little bit too much fun learning, but I did learn. I found that I was talented. My good qualities shined and people started to compliment me on my work, my looks, and my bubbling personality. This was all so new to me. It sure was a boost to my ego.

I enjoyed dating but there really was only one man that I dated that struck me as someone who I would ever consider as a serious partner in life. He had been through a divorce. He had two children and we became very good friends over the next couple of years.

I was totally comfortable with him, but we kept the children out of our relationship the first time around. They were already confused enough and it would have just complicated everything if things did not turn out.

Well, one day he came to me and he had decided that I needed to date other people just to see what it was like. He had been divorced longer than I was. I think he was just scared to death of the "love" word. Anyway, I went along with him and started to date and date and date. Every guy that I dated was compared to him. I just really knew he was the one for me.

After months of dating, one summer night my phone rang. I never expected the voice at the other end to be him. I was so happy but really surprised. He wondered if I would like to go to dinner. You didn't have to ask me twice. We talked and caught up on what we had been doing. I wasn't sure what this meant, but I was hoping it was a good thing.

In October of 1989, I changed jobs. My new job was so much fun and the atmosphere was just so wonderful. It helped tremendously to love my work. I went home at night in a good mood and it reflected in my children's attitude toward me. I worked for the best employers in the world. They are still close to me and my boss has turned out to be my best friend in the world. She is always there for me, a very good listener, and I just love to spend time with her.

I became inside sales manager and office manager. I had twenty-four people reporting to me with twenty-four very different and unique personalities. I cared about each of them and took everything very personally about my job. Sometimes I took the problems home. This was not good for my health, but that is just the type of person I am. Every day was a "trip," as I would day. I never knew what to expect. I never got the things done that I planned on doing for the day. As long as I knew this was the case, it didn't upset me.

In December of 1989, my friend and I were still dating. He lived in another town and I lived in the town where I worked. I was getting tired of being alone. I really was ready to settle down. I also wanted a male figure to support me with my children.

I got very brave one day and gave him his ultimatum. I told him that he could go home and think about our relationship and if we meant as much to each other as he said we did, he could come back with a decision on what his plans were for the future. It was obvious that I wanted him in my life and he knew that. He just needed time to think.

After the holidays that year, he came to visit and he said that he was ready for whatever we needed to do to make our relationship work. We were married in May of 1990.

7.

A Second Chance

I had a fresh new start with someone who truly loved me for who I am. Getting remarried was the scariest thing I have ever done. Those of you who have been married and remarried can understand that.

The evening before the wedding, I broke out into this terrible rash. I called the doctor and he said to come right down. When I got there, he asked if there was anything stressful happening in my life. I told him that I was being remarried the next day. He just laughed and laughed. He told me to enjoy the evening and have a great wedding day. It was purely nerves!

My boys and I were already settled into a mobile home which sat on ten wooded acres. It was just beautiful and we decided that we would stay in my hometown. The mobile home was a beautiful home, just right for the boys and me. Then, we started adding his belongings, a siberian husky and his two pre-teen children on weekends.

It was like a packed can of sardines and we were the sardines. It wasn't long before we were looking at house plans and starting to think about building. We built a beautiful cedar chalet which was perfect for the wooded setting. It was great because it gave all of the children a fresh start in a new home. It was exactly what we hoped for. Life was so good now.

I was the happiest person in the world. I had a great family, a wonderful job, and a wonderful home until one morning in December of 1996.

We had been in the house for several years and I never thought about locking doors where we were located. It was secluded but it was also out in the country.

We had been getting hang up telephone calls very consistently for about one month so we ordered a caller ID from the telephone company. Many of the neighbors noticed a van parked in various locations along our road. It was hunting season so we really did not give it much thought.

This was the period of my life where I was really starting to slide downhill with the Fibromyalgia. I continued to work, thinking that it would just eventually go away.

I woke up on a Monday morning, two weeks before Christmas, with a terrible migraine. I got migraines so much before I started my new program that you will learn about later. I am sure that many of you can relate to these as they are a symptom of Fibromyalgia.

My normal routine was to turn the news on, make my breakfast, let the dog up out of the basement, and get ready for work. I was not driving, so my boss picked me up each morning around 9:00 AM.

I just was feeling so bad that I thought that I would hop in the shower and see if the shower would help my migraine. If I still felt terrible, I was going to have to call off work.

I got into the shower, just standing there letting the warm water run on my aching head and breathing in the steam. All of a sudden, I thought that I heard the phone ring but I let it go, thinking the answering machine would get it.

Then, I heard what sounded like a police or fireman scanner. I shut off the shower thinking to myself, "Oh my word, the house is on fire." But I waited for a little bit and heard two men talking. The one man said, "Wow, we have so much work to do. We better get busy."

By now, I realized that there was no fire. We were being robbed! Every present for every member of our family was under the tree in our family room. All of our computer equipment was in the family room. That is where I thought the voices were. So, now I had to decide what to do.

They did not know that I was in the house and I did not want to surprise them. I had always been told to make noise and get to a safe place. I counted to three, opened the glass shower door, and slammed it as hard as I could.

Then I ran to our adjoining bedroom and slammed that door as hard as I could. I stopped dead in my tracks and listened. There was no more noise. I had no idea where they were in the house or if they had fled the house. You know the old saying "Scared Stiff"? Well, now I know where it came from. I could not move my arms or my legs. I was frozen in place.

After about ten minutes, I got the courage to go to the phone.

Moving my hand to the phone took about five minutes. Dialing my father's number took another ten minutes. My father lived close and he said that he would be right up.

I waited until I heard someone coming in the house. He came to my bedroom door and knocked and said who he was. I just didn't trust that is was him. He kept telling me to open the door. Finally, I did and just fell into his arms.

He searched the house while I called the police and my husband. Whoever was in the house was long gone. Fortunately, they did not have time to steal anything but it didn't matter at that point if they had taken the presents and the tree! I was just glad to be safe.

The police came and started asking me questions. It wasn't until my boss came and the police were questioning me that I broke down. I could not stop crying and I could not go out into the family room. I felt like I had been raped.

After the incident, the neighbors came forward and said that the day before the break-in they had seen two men walking up our driveway while we were at church. They did not connect anything and really felt bad that they had not called us. I really don't think it would have mattered. The next weeks were very difficult for me. I was not sleeping at all. I would just lay there and listen for odd sounds all night long. Finally, I told my husband that I wasn't sure that I could live in the house anymore. We weighed our options, and we finally decided to have a security system installed. It did help but I always felt unsafe in that home.

We have since moved and rebuilt a ranch home which is wonderful. It is great to be closer to the road and out in the open. I still keep the doors locked but I feel much safer.

Now, I am going to end with a funny story that happened while we were still living in the house in the woods. Every morning, I drove my boys down our six hundred and fifty foot drive to meet the school bus. Then I would take off for work.

This one particular morning, I had so many things to do and so many things on my mind. I was also having problems driving. I had backed into the side of a car in town a couple of weeks prior to this incident. I had also passed out driving and was lucky enough to feel it coming on, so was able to pull over to the side of the road before going completely out. It was time to make a decision about my driving anymore, but it is a very difficult thing to give up. You lose your freedom, independence, and most of all so much of your pride.

Well, I made up my mind in a hurry this particular morning. I went to back up and bam, I hit something very solid. I turned around to see the look on my boys' faces. They did not know whether to laugh or cry.

I looked behind me and I could not believe what I hit. I hit a one hundred year old maple tree that had been there every day we lived in the house. What was going on? How could I be so stupid? The first words out of my mouth were, "Who put that thing there?"

Well you can imagine my boys. They were rolling on the floor but it really wasn't so funny. I did not feel competent and I most certainly did not want to hurt the children or any other person or persons for that matter. So, I made the decision to quit driving in December of 1995. I still am not driving. After my heart surgery I plan on trying again.

8.

Losing Someone You Love So Much

I was sitting at work one day and the phone rang. I answered and it was my sister. I could tell that she was crying and I was instantly upset. She broke the news to me that my mom had breast cancer. She had chosen to keep it her little secret and it was in the fourth stage. I was devastated. My mom and dad were my rocks during my whole life. I just thought they were invincible and nothing would ever happen to them. This was my wake up call.

She had a broken back from the cancer in the bones and she just did not want to talk about it. She just wanted to live life while she was still able to. She went through three rounds of intense chemotherapy. I never saw my mother sick. She never got sick. This was very difficult for me to digest.

She was a real trooper though. One day she called me at work to give me more news. The oncologist felt that something else was wrong with her. They did a bone marrow test and found that she also had multiple myeloma which is a bone marrow cancer. So, not only was she dealing with breast cancer but now she was dealing with multiple myeloma. They explained to us that this is a most excruciating, debilitating type of cancer. I just fell apart. I would have rather had it be me. I didn't want to see my mom go through this, but that was not an option.

My dad and mom went on a couple of trips when she had up time and we could see as time went on that she was losing her legs. One day before Christmas of 1991, I was getting lunch and she just could not even get to the bathroom. I told dad we needed to call the doctor. The doctor told us to bring her right in to the hospital.

After work the next day, I went in to see her with the thought that they would help her and she would be home for Christmas. Well, I was sick when they told me that my mom was paralyzed from the waist down. She would never walk again and we could bring her home for Christmas in an ambulance. We would have to have a hospital bed and Hospice would be coming to take care of her daily. I said, "What do you mean, hospice is coming?" The doctor put his arm around me and said that my mom would probably live until sometime in February. I was devastated. I fell into a deep depression. It was so fast, but not really. I just never expected to hear that prognosis on that particular day.

It was Christmas. We should be celebrating, and instead we were all like zombies. I decided that I was going to do something very special for her homecoming. My mom had always wanted a border in her beautiful kitchen, so for therapy, I put up the border before she got home from the hospital.

When they brought her through the door, she looked up and just started to cry. She told them to stop and she just looked all around and said thank you so much. This was the best Christmas present ever. She saw the kitchen only one more time at Easter when we wheeled her in to the living room on a gurney. Yes, I said Easter.

Now it was April of 1992, and my mother was still alive, very alive in spirit, just her body was deteriorating. Easter was the best day she had from the time she came home at Christmas to the time she passed away. She just enjoyed everything about that day.

The caretaking was very intense. Hospice came every day. After work, I went every night and got their dinner. Then, I bathed and prepared my mother for bed. I never got home in the evenings until around 9:00 PM. My wonderful and understanding husband cooked every night, helped the boys with their homework, and made sure they had their showers.

I did this during the week every evening. On the weekends my father was just exhausted, so I stayed overnight for the weekends. I slept in the doorway of the bedroom where my mom was so that my dad could get much needed sleep. I set my clock for every hour to override her morphine pump and give her extra morphine. The pain was excruciating and she was on the highest doses allowed.

This also meant that because I lived the closest, if she needed help in the night, I got up and went down to help dad clean her up. I was not sleeping, eating or functioning properly. Are you starting to see a really bad pattern developing?

In May, we decided as a family that we would rotate nights. There were five of us children and one of us would stay overnight with my Dad every night in case something would happen. We did not want him to be alone.

It was May 19, 1992. I was in charge of my boss's birthday party at work, it was my Nana's (mom's mother) death date, and I was just dragging. The phone rang at 5:30 AM. It was my oldest brother who had stayed the night before. He said that I needed to come right down. Mom was thrashing in pain and he did not know what to do.

I got there and she just looked up at me and said, "Please help me". I told her I would. I boosted her morphine pump and there was no difference. I gave her a valium suppository and nothing helped. I called our Hospice nurse and said that we needed to call the doctor. I was panicking and mom was desperate. This was at 6:00 a.m. At 9: 00 a.m. all of the family had gathered.

For some reason, when the phone rang, I answered it. It was the oncologist and our nurse. They needed to walk me through opening the pump and giving her a huge dose of morphine. I knew in my mind what the consequence would be, but I didn't care at this point. I just wanted my mom to be out of pain. I followed their instructions. Within minutes, she was peaceful and she passed away shortly after.

I wish that I was not the one who did the procedure because it haunts me to this day, but I am glad that my mom has joined my Nana up in heaven.

This was the beginning of the end of my health. I was about to start crashing.

9.

The Downhill Slide Into Fibromyalgia

After my mother died in May of 1992, I started to feel achy and tired all the time. I blamed it on a bad heart valve which I still have. After a few months, I decided to go to a rheumatologist to see if there was something more serious going on.

After an examination and several blood workups, he told me that he felt that I had Fibromyalgia. My first words out of my mouth were, "Fibro what?" I had never heard of this disease. He explained that I showed all of the symptoms, and he also explained to me that there was no cure because they do not know what the real cause is. I was to avoid stress, get plenty of rest, and slow down. Sure, that was going to happen!

I went back to work full speed ahead. We were revamping our entire office at the time so I worked long hours with my boss. I tried to do anything I could to avoid mourning my mother's death. I just missed her so much.

While my mom was sick, I had talked to our church minister about becoming the Music Coordinator for the church. I put it on hold, but after my mom died, I dove in head first. Maybe that is what happened. I must have landed on my head and injured my rational thinking!

I was music coordinator, children's choir director, bell choir director, played the organ for two services every Sunday morning and taught Senior High Sunday School with my friend. What on earth was I thinking? Obviously, I wasn't.

In May of 1986, we were facing another devastating loss in our lives. I got a call at work on a Monday morning. My husband's father had a major stroke and my husband wanted me to come straight from work to the hospital. It was a shock because he was so healthy but he was 84 years old. He suffered for many weeks in the hospital.

Sometimes our hope was high and sometimes we were not sure what was going to happen. After three weeks in the hospital, we had to move him to a nursing home here locally. Deep down, I think that is when he gave up on living.

Meanwhile, my husband's sister had told us at the hospital that her right side was aching but not to worry. She had an appointment with her doctor and she would let us know what she found out. Within a week, we found out that she had ovarian cancer and was hospitalized at the same time, in the same hospital as her father. This was just more than we could bear.

She went through chemotherapy but really never regained her full strength. On May 29th, 1996, we lost Terry's father. This was a major setback for his sister. She just kept going downhill and in October of 1996 we lost her to ovarian cancer. These were the only two living immediate relatives that were alive on my husband's side of the family and we lost them both within months of each other.

My husband's mom had passed away when he was only five years old. I was devastated because I was close to both of them and I was devastated for my husband because he was feeling so many emotions. We made it through, but you can only imagine what this was doing to me physically and mentally. I was just winding down like a battery losing its charge.

I kept on going, getting achy and more worn down as the weeks, months and years passed. Sometimes, I would just sit at my desk at work and the pain would override my thinking ability. I was a walking zombie, and a sick one at that.

By December of 1996, I knew that I was in trouble. I was forgetting messages. I was blanking out completely on jobs that I was supposed to do. It was terrible and very frightening.

I visited my family doctor two weeks before Christmas that year. He said, I think it is time for new blood work and I would like to send you to another rheumatologist. After all of the blood work came back, I was diagnosed with Chronic Fatigue Syndrome and Fibromyalgia. Surprise, surprise!

My doctor said that I needed to drop some of my extracurricular activities and slow the boat down. Being a type "A" personality, that was a very difficult thing for me to accept but I had no choice. My body was giving out.

I went to my boss with the news. I told her that I was not doing justice to my job or the company the way that I was. She did not want me to leave so we tried everything. We lightened my work load. Then, I went part time, only working in the mornings. By May of 1997, I just decided that I needed to quit work. I was not doing a good job and I always strived to do the best work possible. It was making me much more ill to stay and not do justice to my job.

It was one of the saddest times since my mother's death. My boss and I cried and cried. She brought me home and there I was, jobless and sicker than a dog! My boss was so good to me. The company put me on permanent disability and I was hoping that over time I would heal and be able to return to work.

I went from doctor to doctor and test to test and fortunately there was nothing else wrong. For the first time in my life I felt as hopeless as could be. No one could fix me this time. Some of the tests were for some very scary diseases, but with a disease like Fibromyalgia, everything serious must be eliminated to determine that this is truly what you have.

10.

I Tried Everything That Hit the Market

With no cure and very little knowledge of what worked on Fibromyalgia, I continued to visit the rheumatologist. I went through three months of extensive physical therapy which made me feel worse than before I started.

None of the medications were doing anything so I stopped taking all of them. I saw my cardiologist at Cleveland Clinic in October of 1997. He stopped dead in his tracks when he saw me. I had been seeing him for nine years at the time so he knew me well. He said, "What on earth happened to you?" I told him the diagnosis. He decided to run further tests. By the time I was done testing, I felt like they knew every inch of my body and didn't have a clue what to do with me.

I weighed ninety eight pounds. I looked like a cancer patient. I was weak and tired all of the time. I really thought that I was going to die.

After running out of doctors, I started to get really scared. I had frozen shoulders, could barely walk, and was so weak that I really did not leave the house for anything.

I have to tell you this story. It is funny now but it was devastating to me at the time. My birthday is in October and my husband asked me what I wanted for my birthday. I told him that I just wanted new underwear and bras so that when I went to the doctor, I would not be embarrassed. Some birthday present, huh?

Well, my husband and the boys thought they were being really smart. They purchased me a gift certificate to J.C. Penney to buy new underwear. There was just one problem, I could not walk or ride that far. So, I cut out what I wanted from the catalog and asked them to go shopping for me.

Well, this was like asking each one of them to pull out a wisdom tooth! They decided to go in a group. It would be easier to ask. When they got there, I guess, they were each pushing each other up to the counter and finally a nice sales person came up to them and asked if they needed help. My husband said that they needed all of the help that they could get.

As she led them through the underwear department, they said they could feel themselves getting hotter and hotter. They were truly embarrassed. She found what they wanted and bagged it up. When they got home, my husband and the boys said they would never ever set foot in a woman's undergarment department as long as they lived. It is very comical when I look back, but I would have given anything to be able to shop for myself.

Then, there was a miracle. My boss sat on the same board as an infectious disease doctor at the private school where he sent his children. They were talking one evening at a board meeting. My boss was telling him about me. The doctor asked if I had been checked for Lymes Disease. My boss called me and I told him that I had only been tested four times and all of the tests were negative. The doctor still wanted to see me. I set up an appointment and he saw me right away.

He was the kindest doctor that I have ever been to. He was totally in tune to my symptoms. He said that he thought he could help me get back on track. He put me on an antidepressant for depression but also for pain. Antidepressants help Fibromyalgia pain. He also put me on a sleeping medication because he felt that my sleep was being interrupted by the pain and he wanted me to get into a better sleep pattern.

Within weeks, I was gaining weight, sleeping better and the pain was much less intense. He worked with me for months and then set me up with a group of doctors. They included an internist, a neurologist, and a clinical psychologist. Why did I need to see a clinical psychologist? Well, I found out after I started to see her. All of my childhood issues, my first marriage issues, the depression of my mother's death, the devastation of the illness, and so many other things came into play.

I lost a good portion of my short term memory retention, so I started working on the internet to try to keep my brain as active as possible. We worked through all of the other issues and I learned how to deal with them. It was a very positive experience for me.

Just when I thought things might be looking up, another tragedy. My father and I had become very close after I stopped working. I really enjoyed spending time with him. He took me to my physical therapy and we just really shared quality time together.

One day in June of 1997, my stepmother called to say that my father was not okay. He had been having chest pain for two days and pain down his left arm. He had a cardiac history so I tried to persuade him to let me call an ambulance. He was not going to the hospital in an ambulance. He said there were people out there so much more in need and he would drive himself.

My father was a warm hearted man, but a very stubborn man. He did listen to my sister-in-law, though, so I called her right away. She talked him into letting her drive him to the hospital. When we arrived at the hospital, we were going to get him a wheelchair. Oh no, he would walk in the hospital and walk out the same way.

Once they got him settled into a room in the ER, they called his cardiologist down right away. My dad said, "How soon can I leave? We have bowling tonight." The cardiologist just smiled and said, "You will have to miss bowling tonight. You have had a major heart attack, so we will be admitting you for further tests."

My dad was upset, but suddenly became very cooperative. I think it was a combination of relief and he was just plain scared.

We stayed with him until they got him settled in a room and then we all went home. I was so sick and very tired. Little did I know what was to come in the weeks ahead.

They did a catheterization and found that he was 99% blocked in his main artery and all of the other main arteries had blockage as well. He was too weak to do bypass surgery, so they went in and put a stint in the main artery to alleviate the pain from the heart attack and help the blood flow.

He seemed to be making really good progress. It was the night before Father's Day in 1997. I had a terrible migraine but I knew that I needed to go see my dad. For some reason, I took his Father's Day card with me. I wrote him a letter and asked him to open the card while I was there.

He said he would wait until the next day but I insisted that he open it just in case I was too sick to come in the following day. He appreciated my letter so much. I just wanted him to know how important he was in my life and how much I loved him. I am so glad that I got the chance to say that to him.

The next morning was Father's Day. My boys had a tradition with my husband. They got up early and went golfing every Father's Day. They left around 7:00 a.m.

I really was suffering with my migraine so I laid back down in bed. Around 9:00 the phone rang. It was the hospital. They told me that my father had gone into cardiac arrest and they were moving him to intensive care.

I called my husband off the golf course. He and the boys met me at the hospital. What I saw when I arrived at the hospital was unreal. They had my father hooked up to so many tubes that I really hardly recognized him. It was a very long emotional day.

As the days went on, he was on a rollercoaster ride. They revived him four times. They decided on July 7th to insert a pacemaker to help control the rhythm of his heart. Everything went according to plans. We spoke with the doctor after the procedure and he said how strong my Dad was and that he should do well. We all went home for rest.

The next morning, the phone rang and it was the hospital again. They said that we should gather the family. My father had taken a turn for the worse and we needed to come right away.

We got there and dad was so peaceful. He was barely breathing but quiet and at peace. The priest came in and we said a prayer and he died shortly after.

I was so lost without my dad. I was so used to going to my mom and dad for guidance. Now, they were both gone. The adjustment was so difficult and it really took a toll on my health, especially on the Fibromyalgia.

I just was having such a difficult time and knew that I needed a new approach, but I was just too tired to fight. My health was so poor and I just needed time to heal, to grieve and to try to get some kind of a life back.

In December of 1998, there was another death in my family. My brother-in-law had struggled with diabetes for many years. He was on dialysis and eventually had to be put in a nursing home. It was terrible to see someone that was a brother figure to me all of my life so helpless.

Every time that I went to visit, I came home and sobbed. He lost a foot and leg up to his knee and then that would not heal. Before they went any further, his organs started to shut down and he died.

He was just way too young to be gone, but he was. I miss him every day.

In September of 2000, we had another hard blow. My sister-in-law's father had struggled with esophageal cancer for over two years. He had surgery and struggled to heal from the surgery. Then he bounced back a bit only to go back downhill and never regain his strength. He was my rock after my dad died. We had many long talks about life and how to treat people. He was just such a wonderful man and we lost him on September 2, 2000.

I felt as though my foundation had been rocked over the past few years. Everyone who I went to for advice was gone. All of my mentors were gone. We know that dying is part of the life process, but that doesn't make us any more prepared to lose the people that we love so dearly.

II.

Coming Up With My Own System

After all of the loss, I started to fight back. I felt that is what my family would want me to do. I thought that maybe walking and diet would be a key. Walking helped, but my hips still really hurt and I was unable to do very much cardiovascular exercise because of my faulty Mitral Valve.

I have always been a healthy eater so I tried a few modifications, but that did not seem to make a huge difference since I already ate healthy to begin with.

My weight was a big issue for me. I kept climbing and climbing which made no sense to me, but it was happening. I asked my doctor and he felt it was the antidepressant, Prozac, that was making me gain weight. He tried a couple of other antidepressants but the pain got worse.

Finally, we came up with one that seems to work very well for me. It is called Effexor and actually weight loss is one of the side effects. That was just fine with me. It has balanced my weight out and I am holding steady at one hundred and thirty eight pounds.

You have to remember that diet and exercise have become a big part of my life now, also. The medication is not a magic bullet to weight loss but it does help with my pain and keeps me very level as far as my weight is concerned.

I started to do Tai Chi. I ordered a video set over the internet and it took about one week to see that the squatting and standing was killing my knees. I really found it rather boring, also. But, it probably works for many people. It was just not a good fit for me.

I looked at Pilates but thought that it was a bit too aggressive for me and for anyone with Fibromyalgia.

Finally, I started looking into yoga. I thought that this was something that I might be able to do, but many of the moves were too difficult for me or they just plain hurt. I started to modify the moves and came up with a wonderful and doable exercise plan for me.

Then I thought, "Why don't I develop a program specifically to meet the needs of those of us with Fibromyalgia?" I started to research whether there was such a program out there and came up with rehabilitation therapy programs, exercise for aging, arthritis programs, programs for diabetes.

I only came across one exercise tape that was actually labeled Fibromyalgia yoga. I purchased the tape and started to try the moves. Well, the first move I did was a hip opener and I injured my groin area so bad that I was down for two days. Now I was even more determined to come up with something doable for us fibromyalgians. It was time for me to get to work.

The next chapters are dedicated to my five part program for Fibromyalgia. It includes Fibroga Exercise Movement Therapy for Fibromyalgia, Diet and Nutrition for Fibromyalgia, Fibromyalgia Massage Therapy, Chiropractry for Fibromyalgia and beauty tips to look good and feel better.

12.

Fibroga: Exercise Movement Therapy for Fibromyalgia

Fibroga is my own version of an exercise movement therapy that combines warm up exercises, stretching, and minimal strengthening exercise for people with Fibromyalgia.

It is gentle and safe if done the way it is supposed to be done. It helps to stimulate the flow of blood and oxygen to the brain. It helps to stretch the muscle tension that is associated with Fibromyalgia. It is also a minimal strengthening program with emphasis on minimal. It always ends with complete relaxation of the body so that the muscles are not tense and the body feels refreshed.

The wonderful concept of my program is that you only work the body until you feel the pull, never into any pain. If there is ever pain, you back out immediately.

Not all exercise movements are suitable to every person. We are all made differently. We all have different issues. I guide you through the exercises with great detail and I let you know if you have certain issues in certain areas which exercises you probably should not do.

The first tape is so gentle. Much of it is done from sitting on a chair. Other exercises use the chair as a prop for balance and support. Some exercises are done on the floor but you can also use props such as rolled towels and pillows, etc.

At no time should you ever be uncomfortable. This program is meant to help you gain more flexibility, stamina, and even some strength. It is not meant to harm your body in any way.

The final movement in the exercise therapy is always relaxation. It is a deep inhaling and exhaling through the nose. On the inhale, the stomach and the rib cage expand and on the exhale the stomach tightens pushing the air up and out through the lungs.

In my style of relaxation, we relax different parts of the body on each exhale and inhale. On the exhale, you make the body part heavy and sinking. Then, on the inhale you lighten the body part as if it is floating in the air. This is called Body Scanning and I feel that it works best to breathe with the movement. It keeps your body and mind working together. That is what we are trying to achieve: a body and mind connection.

Did you know that deep inhaling and exhaling burns calories? It also helps your posture. To do the breathing in a correct manner, you must sit up straight or lay down flat to get the best flow of oxygen and blood throughout the body.

Did you know that stretching your muscles actually helps them to relax? That is why I have included stretching of the arms, torso, and legs in my exercise program.

Did you know that moving your arms and legs keeps you from getting frozen shoulders and restless legs? Keeping your body parts still is not the answer to help in the healing of your achy body. Gentle movement is the best thing that you can do for your body.

When I first started developing this exercise therapy, I could barely lift my arms over my head. My legs were weak. I had very little muscle mass. After gradually and consistently doing the exercises each day and then finishing with relaxation, I feel like a new person. Yes, I still have some achy times, but it is nothing like it was before I started the program. I have so much more stamina. I can actually think more clearly because the blood and oxygen are flowing better to my brain and through my body.

I hope that each of you will consider this program. The tapes are easy to follow and my classes are just plain fun. If it isn't fun, who wants to do it, right?

Please come join me. You can purchase my videos/DVDs on my website at www.thegroveapproach.com. Or if you live in the Ohio, Pennsylvania, or New York area, please give me a call for details on class information. It is wonderful to connect personally with others that share our common problems. Sometimes this is the best way to learn about how to deal with our disease. Give it a try. I guarantee that you will have no regrets, just fond memories.

13.

Diet and Nutrition For Healthier Fibromyalgia Living

Diet and nutrition are important to everyone. They are especially important to Fibromyalgia patients because we are so sensitive to different foods and nutrients.

I find it very amazing that there are so many foods that can cause us to have a "fibro attack". A fibro attack can range from muscle aches, to migraine headaches, to urinary complications, to a drop in energy levels, to many of the other symptoms that are associated with the disease. We sure do not need any more complications than we already have.

We need to eat a wide variety of foods, not just our favorites all of the time. Balance and variety are the keys to forming good eating habits.

Many foods that we eat are very good for our health. Fruits such as blueberries, raspberries, strawberries, bananas, cherries, grapes and apples are very good for our diet.

Vegetables such as legumes, beans, carrots, squash, red peppers, (not green peppers-they can trigger a fibro attack), cabbage, spinach and asparagus are very good for us.

There are many meats that are healthy for us, also. Tuna, salmon, white meats such as turkey and fish are all good meat choices for us to eat.

Grains are very important in our diet as well. Oatmeal, whole grain cereal, cereals high in fiber, bran cereals, brown rice, etc, are great grains to be adding to our diets.

What we drink is very, very important. I cannot emphasize the need for our bodies to have fluids, especially water. The best water is purified water. This comes in bottles, a purification system on your water tank, a simple purification system on the end of your water faucet, and some refrigerators even come with a purification system in them so that the water you drink from them is also purified. Ideally, drinking as much water as you feel thirsty for is the norm. Some people drink up to eight glasses of water a day. You can vary your water intake with alternatives such as cranberry juices, natural unsweetened fruit juices, tea (not over excessive because of the caffeine), etc.

After exercising, drinking a sports drink is essential to make sure that your electrolytes stay in balance. Exercising takes a good amount of fluids from your body. Gatorade or any sports drink is good for this.

Green tea is the best tea that you can put in your body. It eliminates caffeine that you find in coffee and dark teas. Caffeine is a very strong irritant to Fibromyalgia patients. If you are going to stop drinking caffeinated coffee and /or caffeinated tea, do this gradually. Start with one half cup and then go every other day, eventually weaning yourself off of it. Going off of it cold turkey can cause other complications such as shaking, upset stomach, migraines and other side effects.

Some foods that we should avoid are called "trigger" foods. They trigger attacks in fibromyalgia patients ranging from digestive problems, headaches, muscle aches, anxiety, fatigue, etc.

Here is just a short list of foods that are bad for you. Please remember that processed foods do contain some of these trigger foods, so be very careful in your selections of processed foods. Some of the trigger foods include: high fat dairy products, fried foods, white sugar (replace with Stevia), white flour (replace with spelt flour), red meats, preservatives, salty foods, coffee, caffeinated teas, soda pop, alcoholic beverages, NutraSweet, saccharine, aspartame, tobacco, corn, an abundance of citrus fruit, and chocolate. Did I hit a couple of nerves?

There are very good substitutes for many of the very high "trigger" foods that we use every day. The health food stores are wonderful places to find these foods and some grocery stores do have organic sections with some of the foods, also.

I just want to touch on a couple of replacements for some of the key ingredients that we use in cooking. These become important as we bake or use them as replacements in recipes.

The first is a replacement for sugar called Stevia. Stevia comes from an herb. Believe it or not, it is up to 15 times sweeter than regular white sugar! This is good news for those of us who like sweets but are also watching our weight. It is very accessible and very inexpensive. Here is an example. To replace one cup of regular white sugar, you would only use 1 to 1 ½ tablespoons of Stevia! Diabetics use it regularly. Give it a try. Help your fibro attacks as well as your waistline.

There are other natural substitutions for sugar. Some include honey, molasses, unsweetened fruit juices, maple syrup and barley malt. The reductions of these are not quite as drastic as the Stevia is but you can experiment with the things that you like and that taste good to you. You can purchase my Fibro Cookbook online at my website at www.thegroveapproach.com.

The second is a replacement for white flour. I chose the staples that we use most frequently to discuss. White flour seems to be used in about everything. But, there is good news. Most health food stores and the organic sections of some grocery stores are carrying substitutes for the white flour. In my research, the closest replacement is called Spelt Flour. It is a grain that is very easily digested. The spelt grain has a more buttery taste but that sounds pretty good to me! It is used just as flour would be. The consistency and amounts are so similar to white flour that you can use the same measurements to replace white flour.

Another staple that we use is wheat flour. Wheat flour, like white flour, is processed and so many of the good nutrients are taken out in the process. There are some very good substitutes for wheat flour. Some include rice flour, corn meal, oat flour, buckwheat flour, and barley flour. For one cup of wheat flour substitute the following: ¾ cup of corn meal, 1 1/3 cups of oat flour, 7/8 cup of buckwheat flour, and 1 1 /3 cup of barley flour.

Did you know that you do need fat in your diet? We should be eating regular butter, not margarine. We should be cooking with olive oil and canola oil.

Did you know that it is better to eat five or six small meals during the day, rather than three major meals? It is so much easier for our stomach to digest smaller amounts of food. It helps you maintain your energy level, to keep you from overeating because you have allowed yourself to get too hungry, and it keeps your metabolism balanced.

Did you ever think that when you go out to dinner there is just too much food for you to eat at one sitting? I suggest asking for a container or doggy bag right away and splitting your meal into two parts. Put one part in the container and it makes a great lunch or dinner for the next day! It has helped me with weight control immensely because my favorite thing to do is eat out!

These are just a few of the things that you will find in my nutrition and diet part of my program. Eating and drinking healthy makes a healthier body. The adjustments are not that difficult and I will make it even easier by providing you with a wonderful cookbook with many of your favorite recipes and some new ones that are simply out of this world!

Remember that taking care of you is taking care of all of you, not just a part of you. Start today towards becoming a healthier you!

14.

Fibromyalgia Massage Therapy

Fibromyalgia Massage Therapy is an area that has to be closely researched before choosing a therapist. There are several questions that you should ask before selecting the therapist.

The first question is "Do you know what Fibromyalgia is?" Make sure that you are positive that they know what it is, what the symptoms are, how it affects your muscles and skeleton, and how you feel when you have Fibromyalgia. If they don't know, then you need to search for another therapist.

The second thing that you need to have them do is to describe in detail their massage technique. I know that this sounds incredibly senseless. You are probably thinking massage is massage. That is not true. A true fibro massage therapist has a very unique technique.

Massage therapists are taught to pull toward the heart center to stimulate the blood flow and circulation. This is exactly what we, as Fibromyalgia patients, do not want. We do not want our muscles to be stimulated. We want them to be relaxed and calm.

A fibro massage therapist will work away from the heart center. They will pull away on your arms, legs, and torso. This is the key to getting your muscles to relax, not to tense up.

The next thing that you need to know is what kind of touch the fibro therapist has. You may not see it as so important, but I can tell you from experience that one thing you do not want is deep tissue massage—and some therapists love to go deep into the muscle. This is definitely a problem to a Fibromyalgia patient. You will feel the pain but just wait until the next day. You can be bruised and very, very sore. This experience should not be miserable. You should come away refreshed and rejuvenated.

Also, a good fibro massage therapist will use moist heat either during or after your massage. This relaxes you and just helps to settle down the nerve endings that the therapist has just worked on.

I would recommend a visit to the salon prior to your therapy. You have the right to check out the facility. The most important thing to look for at the salon is cleanliness. Because we are so susceptible to bacterial and viral infections, check the sheets and bedding, the room cleanliness, and I usually go to the restroom. The restroom at any public facility is usually a very good indicator of the cleanliness of the facility.

Another thing to watch for, which you will not know until the therapist does your first massage, is that they are there to serve you. Chatting is good, but the chat should be focused on you. If the therapist is talking all about his or her problems, that sure is not going to help you relax and it most certainly is not going to help you keep a positive attitude. If you really like the therapist, just very nicely ask them if they could not talk at all. Let the therapist know that you really like to get into your mind and body while having a massage. They should understand. If they don't understand, you need to find a new therapist.

I am sure that you never thought that shopping for a therapist could be so detailed, but it is very important that you connect in a positive way with your therapist. So, start checking those therapists out and good luck!

15.

Chiropractic Approach to Fibromyalgia

There are many people with Fibromyalgia turning to chiropractic approach. It is a drug free alternative and it does get results.

The chiropractor's role is to help free you from a severe form of stress found in your spine. These are called vertebral subluxations or VS. VS are distortions of your spine and body structure that stress your brain, spinal cord, nerves, joints, ligaments, muscles, internal organs and other tissues. They cause disturbed body function, loss of wholeness, lowered resistance to disease, lack of energy, loss of height and premature aging. Over hundreds of years of clinical observations have revealed that vertebral subluxations can affect your physical and mental health. (Wolf, Anderson, Harkes, 1997).

In a study published by *The American Journal of Medicine*, research showed that 45.9% of people who had fibromyalgia and went to a chiropractor experienced moderated to great improvement. (Wolf, 1986) These are amazing results. I see a chiropractor and it really helps to keep my spine in line.

Many of you are probably saying, "Oh, I just don't like the cracking and popping of my joints and bones." Believe me, I don't either. They have new instruments now where they just push them against the spine and you don't feel or hear anything except the click of the instrument. I would not be going if I had to listen to those sounds. If you are looking for a chiropractor, make sure to ask if they do treatment that does not involve cracking of bones.

You also need to ask to make sure that they are experienced with fibromyalgia patients. Just ask them if they know what fibromyalgia is and you will know if you have chosen the correct chiropractor or not. There are many chiropractors who work with only fibromyalgia patients now because it gives such remarkable relief to most patients. If you are interested in reading more about chiropractors

and fibromyalgia, please visit my website at www.thegroveapproach
.com.

16.

Me Time: Looking Good, Feeling Good

Ever since my mother was ill, the phrase "Looking Good, Feeling Good" sticks in my mind at all times. I was always taught to take care of myself, especially grooming. My mom made sure that my hair was set every night and that my clothes were clean and pressed. She always wanted us to look our best, no matter where we were going.

My father used to get terribly upset with me because I did not feel that it was proper to leave the house with curlers in my hair. Somehow, I felt like I still had my PJ's on!

It has stayed with me for life, except when I first got sick. I do not leave the house without a clean and presentable outfit on, my hair styled, and my make-up on. If I ever did, I would feel like I was leaving the house naked!

I am sure that many of you can relate. The only time that I broke this trend was when I became ill. I just really didn't care what I looked like. I let my hair go, I didn't wear make-up, and I really did not care what I was wearing as long as it covered my miserable body!

Over the first couple of years, people looked at me and would ask, "What happened to you? Are you really sick?"

I started to feel so self-conscious that I would just stay in as much as possible, only going out if I absolutely had to. It was just really difficult to get ready to go places. I was worn out just from getting a shower and getting dressed!

After about five years, I started to feel like I wanted to get a new outfit now and then. I don't know what it is about putting on something new, but I actually felt better physically and about myself. I always loved to shop for clothes and did most of my shopping on the internet. I still do.

Then I decided it was time to style my hair so I started going to the hairdresser and once I started, I kept going back on a regular basis. It felt so much better after she cut and styled it for me.

Next, I started to wear a little make-up again. Wow, what a difference a little make-up can do. I felt like a new person. I was still exhausted getting ready to go out, but at least people were not staring at me and thinking, "You poor thing, how long do you have left?".

My husband and I decided that we needed to find a hobby that both of us could be involved in. We knew that it could not be real physical and that it could not be something really challenging. We both have a passion for old things. I started investigating antique and collectable glassware and vintage linens. He started to collect Coca Cola memorabilia.

We went to estate sales which are very popular in this region. You take a number and then wait for your number to be called. The wait is usually not too long. Then, you go through the home and look at the items on display. They are all tagged with prices. If you want to purchase something, you just pick it up and pay for it and it is yours!

Over the past years, it has been our time together. We got to one or two sales and then we have lunch together. We needed something to connect us outside of the home and this has worked wonderfully.

Try to come up with a list of some ideas for things that you would like to do with others or with your spouse and pick one that you really have a passion for. It is really good to get out with others and it makes you feel more like a normal part of society.

I think that "me time" is also very important in the healing process of fibromyalgia. After all, most of us got in this situation by overdoing, usually for others. So, now take some "me time". To me, it is time to just do what you enjoy. Maybe it is reading a book, sitting a bubble bath with candles, going out and getting your nails done, getting a new hair style, shopping for a new outfit, going out to lunch with a friend or your spouse, or whatever you just really enjoy doing.

The thing that you need to remember is that "me time" is in no way selfish! Healthy people should have "me time". There would be so many less sick people in this world.

I can testify that doing these things or doing just even one of these things will help not only your positive attitude, but it will also help your healing process. It will bring you back in touch with the real world and it will give you a sense of being. Everyone needs to have a sense of self-worth and being.

Don't wait. Don't put this off. Start this process today, the first day of the rest of your life. Plan what are the most important things that you would like to accomplish in life. Life is very short, so don't waste any more time.

Look at me. Who would have ever thought that FIBROGA, diet and nutrition, massage therapy, fibromyalgia chiropractry and beauty tips would spark me to start my own business at the age of fifty? If I can do it, so can you. I have walked in your shoes and you have walked in mine. We really understand each other.

Life is a journey and please don't leave any pages blank. If you ever want to talk, please feel free to go to my website and we can talk on line or I can call you. Again, my website address is thegroveapproach.com.

My wish for each of you is for better health, loving people to surround you, peace in your body and mind, and joy in your heart. The best of everything to each of you, my fibromyalgia friends!

References

Wolf F, Anderson J, Harkness D et Al. Prospective, longitudinal study of service utilization and costs in fibromyalgia. *Arthritis and Rheumatism*, 1997;40:1560-1570.

Wolfe F. The clinical syndrome of fibrositis. *American Journal of Medicine*. 1986;81(suppl 3A):7-14.